THE TECHNOLOGY OF
HOCKEY

by Shane Frederick

HIGH-TECH SPORTS

CAPSTONE PRESS
a capstone imprint

Sports Illustrated Kids High-Tech Sports are published by Capstone Press,
1710 Roe Crest Drive, North Mankato, Minnesota 56003
www.capstonepub.com

SI Kids is a trademark of Time Inc. Used with permission.

Library of Congress Cataloging-in-Publication Data
Frederick, Shane.
  The technology of hockey / by Shane Frederick.
      p. cm.—(Sports illustrated kids. High-tech sports)
  Includes bibliographical references and index.
  Summary: "Discusses the forms of technology that has revolutionized the game of hockey"
—Provided by publisher.
  ISBN 978-1-4296-9954-9 (library binding)
  ISBN 978-1-62065-912-0 (paperback)
1. Hockey—Juvenile literature. I. Title.
  GV847.25.F738 2013
  796.962—dc23   2012033674

Editorial Credits
Anthony Wacholtz, editor; Veronica Scott, designer; Eric Gohl, media researcher;
Eric Manske production specialist

Photo Credits
Alamy: www.maximimages.com, 41, ZUMA Press, Inc., 29;
AP Images: *The Canadian Press*/Darren Calabrese, 30, *The Canadian Press*/Frank
Gunn, 8, *The Canadian Press*/Richard Lam, 15 (top), Dan Loh, 43, Reed Saxon, 21 (inset); Courtesy of
Applied Cognitive Engineering (ACE)/IntelliGym: 23; Getty Images: Christian Petersen, 31, Jim Prisching,
17, NHL/Rick Stewart, 19, NHLI/Dave Reginek, 32, NHLI/Dave Sandford, 38, NHLI/Jeff Vinnick, 39, NHLI/
Rob Marczynski, 36 (inset), NHLI/Scott Audette, 40; Landov: MCT/*Detroit Free Press*/Julian H. Gonzalez,
25; Library of Congress: 6; Newscom: EPA/John G. Mabanglo, 24, Icon SMI/Leon T. Switzer, 20–21, Icon
SMI/Patrick S. Blood, 35, Icon SMI/Shelly Castellano, 5, iPhoto Inc./Jana Chytilova, 27, ZUMA Press,
26; Shutterstock: Dmitriy Shironosov, cover (background), 1; *Sports Illustrated*: Bob Martin, 33, Damian
Strohmeyer, 22, 28, David E. Klutho, 7 (top), 10, 11, 13 (bottom), 15 (bottom), 16, 18, 34, 36–37, 42, Hy
Peskin, 13 (top), John W. McDonough, cover, 14, Robert Beck, 7 (bottom), 9, 12, 44–45, Simon Bruty, 4
Design Elements: Shutterstock

Printed in the United States of America in Stevens Point, Wisconsin.
092012   006937WZS13

TABLE OF CONTENTS

HOCKEY: AN EVOLVING GAME

Zdeno Chara had a new stick, and he couldn't wait to see what it could do. The Boston Bruins defenseman and team captain took it out on the ice for the 2012 NHL All-Star Skills Competition. He hoped to defend his title for the fastest shot that he won in 2011. Using a lightweight but super-strong and flexible stick made of carbon fiber, Chara raced down the ice toward the puck. He pulled back his stick and swung it down at the puck, rocketing the rubber disk toward an empty goal. The scoreboard posted the puck's speed: 108.8 miles (175 kilometers) per hour—almost 3 miles (4.8 km) per hour faster than his previous record!

Zdeno Chara

Who could have imagined such a shot 150 years ago? The origins of the game of hockey go back that far with skaters playing a game on frozen ponds and rivers with wooden sticks. By the late 1800s, the first rules were written down and clubs began to form. The Stanley Cup was presented as a championship prize in 1893, and it's still awarded to the National Hockey League champions today.

Much about the game has changed since then. The rules have evolved, the players have grown bigger and stronger, and the equipment has improved. Tens of thousands of people fill arenas every weekend to watch games live, and millions more watch on television. Technology and engineering have altered the way players train for the game, where they play, the way coaches run their teams, and the way fans watch.

TV announcers and commentators sit in booths that allow them to see the entire rink.

While certain things about today's game are the same as in hockey's early days, many aspects would be unrecognizable to time-traveling hockey players from the past. High-tech sticks, ice-making equipment, and instant replay might make them think they're watching a sport on another planet.

Let's see how technology has made hockey what it is today.

CHAPTER 1

EVOLUTION OF THE STICK

Whether you're playing ice hockey, field hockey, floor hockey, or roller hockey, one piece of equipment is always in use: the stick. Over the history of the game, hockey sticks have changed a lot, thanks to technology.

Princeton hockey team from the early 1900s

In the early years, sticks were carved out of single pieces of wood, usually from maple, willow, or ash trees. Over time players wanted to get more out of their sticks. They wanted them lighter, stronger, more flexible, and more accurate. Companies experimented with various materials, including laminated layers of wood in the 1940s and aluminum sticks in the 1980s.

Today's high-tech composite sticks are made of combinations of graphite, **Kevlar**, fiberglass, and **titanium**. The strong, flexible shafts allow shooters to fire wicked wristers and rocket slap shots.

Companies use technology to test out their new designs and make sure their sticks are ready for anything. That technology includes puck-shooting robots and stick-breaking machines.

Katie King of the U.S. Olympic team

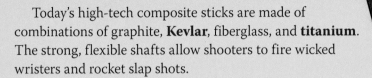

TAKE OUT THE BOUNCE

NHL hockey pucks are made of vulcanized rubber—a rubber mixed with sulfur at high temperatures to make it stronger. Pucks are frozen before use to prevent them from bouncing too much on the ice.

Kevlar—a high-strength material
titanium—a very strong and light metal

SKATES: GETTING AN EDGE

People have skated on ice for thousands of years. At first they used animal bones as skate blades. Eventually wood and metal were used to glide across frozen lakes and rivers.

THE HEAT IS ON

Hockey players are always looking for a competitive advantage. One inventor thought that a warm skate blade would help players skate faster. The ThermaBlade has a battery-powered heater that warms the blade to 40 degrees Fahrenheit (4 degrees Celsius). Water freezes at 32 F (0 C), so the blade melts the ice into a thin layer of water, making the ice slicker under the skate.

Hockey players today wear skates with steel blades. In order to skate effectively, players must have the blades sharpened with a grinding stone. Each blade has two razor-sharp edges with a hollow carved-out section between them. Skaters use those edges to grip the ice to start, stop, and turn. A dull edge can slow a player down or even cause him or her to fall. NHL players have their skates sharpened every day. Some even have them sharpened between periods of a game.

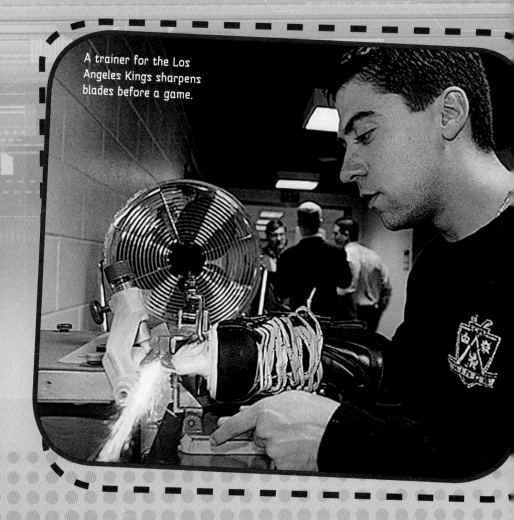

A trainer for the Los Angeles Kings sharpens blades before a game.

PROTECTING THE HEAD

The NHL began requiring players to wear helmets in 1979. But the league allowed players already in the league at that point to have the choice. Craig MacTavish chose to play without a helmet. When he retired in 1997 with the St. Louis Blues, he was the last player in the league to play without head protection.

Sidney Crosby

Even with helmets, head injuries remained a serious concern. In 1968 the Minnesota North Stars' Bill Masterton was knocked down and hit his head on the ice. He died two days later. Because of two **concussions**, Pittsburgh Penguins superstar Sidney Crosby missed 41 games in 2010–11 and only played 22 games in 2011–12.

concussion—an injury to the brain caused by a hit to the head

Research is constantly being done to improve helmets in order to curb head injuries, especially concussions. Helmets now consist of a hard, lightweight plastic shell with foam padding inside. While they can't completely prevent concussions, they can absorb and transfer the energy from a hit into the boards or a fall to the ice.

A helmet cage protects Canadian Olympian Jennifer Botterill's face.

Hall of Famer Mark Messier is involved in a project to make helmets even better. His helmets have shock-absorbing cylinders between the shell and the foam. The cylinders instantly compress on impact to absorb the blow. They also bounce back just as quickly so the helmet—and the player—are ready for the next hit.

STOPPING THE PUCK

The bravest athletes in all of sports might be hockey goaltenders. The puck can hurtle toward the goaltender at more than 100 miles (161 km) per hour! Goalies use technology to make their job easier and safer.

A goaltender's enormous leg pads were once made of leather. Today they are made of stronger, lighter **synthetic** material. The new material doesn't get weighed down when it absorbs water from the melting ice.

Jonathan Quick

synthetic—not natural, made by combining different substances

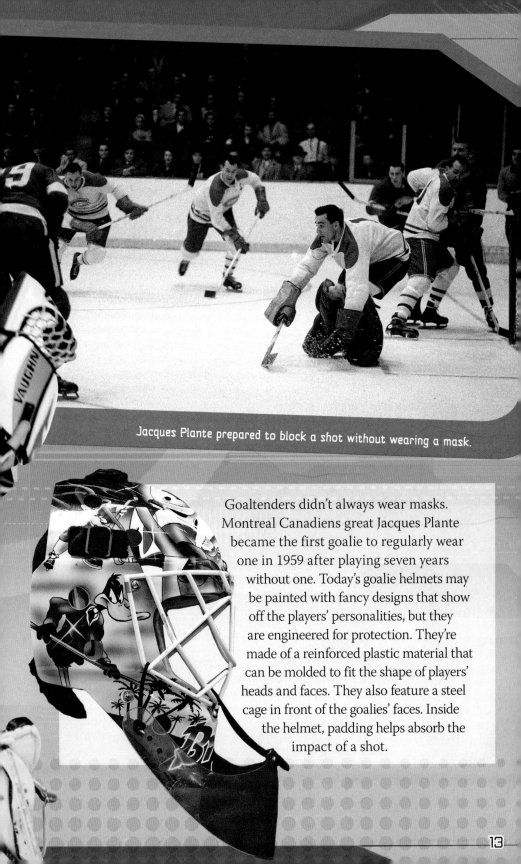

Jacques Plante prepared to block a shot without wearing a mask.

Goaltenders didn't always wear masks. Montreal Canadiens great Jacques Plante became the first goalie to regularly wear one in 1959 after playing seven years without one. Today's goalie helmets may be painted with fancy designs that show off the players' personalities, but they are engineered for protection. They're made of a reinforced plastic material that can be molded to fit the shape of players' heads and faces. They also feature a steel cage in front of the goalies' faces. Inside the helmet, padding helps absorb the impact of a shot.

INSIDE ICE

If you've been to a hockey arena, you may have wondered how it could be warm at your seat but cold enough to keep the ice frozen inside the boards. Or maybe you've wondered why the ice doesn't melt in Los Angeles or Miami or during warm June nights when the Stanley Cup is being decided.

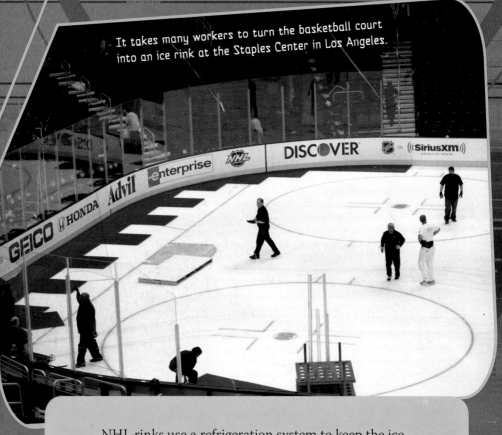

It takes many workers to turn the basketball court into an ice rink at the Staples Center in Los Angeles.

NHL rinks use a refrigeration system to keep the ice playable at all times. Underneath the ice is a concrete floor with as much as 5 miles (8 km) of pipes inside. The pipes are pumped with brine, a liquid that can be chilled well below freezing. Layers of water flood the rink, and the cold floor turns them to ice. It takes from 12,000 to 15,000 gallons (45,400 to 56,800 liters) of water to form an ice rink.

Crew members of the 2010 Winter Olympics in Vancouver, British Columbia, checked the refrigeration pipes running underneath a rink.

KEEPING THE ICE SMOOTH

During a game players' skate blades slice through the ice, scratching it, chipping it, and making it a slower surface. By the end of a period of play, the cut-up, snowy ice makes it tough to skate, pass, and shoot. Arenas use ice-resurfacing machines to freshen up the ice regularly. As the huge vehicles slowly circle the rink, they shave off a layer of ice with a sharp blade and collect the "snow" in a holding tank. Then they wash the ice and suck away the dirty water. Finally they spread a thin layer of clean water that freezes on the surface. Voila! A sleek sheet is ready for the next period.

THE BOARDS AND GLASS

Dasher boards surround hockey rinks to keep pucks in play (most of the time) and still allow fans to see all of the action. They're also a big part of the game itself. Players often deliver big body checks, slamming their opponents into the boards.

Sometimes those checks can lead to injuries, including broken arms, separated shoulders, and serious head and neck trauma. While rules and equipment have changed to cut down those injuries, engineers have tried to make the boards safer too.

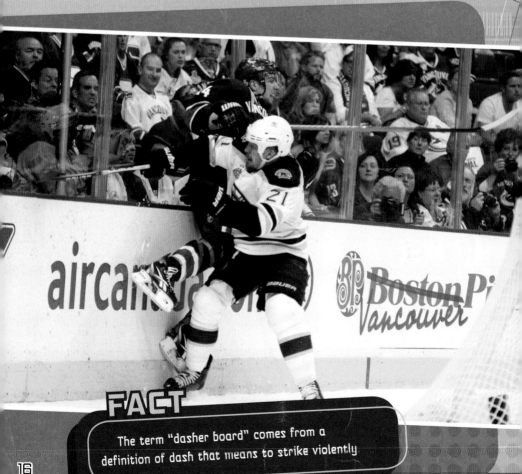

FACT

The term "dasher board" comes from a definition of dash that means to strike violently

NHL rinks now have flexible boards complete with shock absorbers inside. They give way and absorb energy when a collision occurs so it's not like hitting a brick wall.

The glass above the boards is either an acrylic material, such as **Plexiglas**, or tempered glass. Tempered glass is a hard, strong glass created through a heating process. Like car windows, if the glass is broken, it shatters into tiny dull pieces rather than dangerous shards. Plasticlike acrylic "glass" is more flexible and absorbs energy better than tempered glass. The acrylic material is used in the corners and ends of NHL rinks in order to better protect players from hard hits into the boards. Some NHL teams use acrylic glass all the way around their rinks.

Plexiglas—a strong, clear plastic that can substitute for regular glass

Members of the ice crew replace one of the Plexiglas panes above the boards.

TAKING IT BACK OUTSIDE

Hockey began outdoors on frozen ponds and rivers before moving inside to arenas. In 2003 the NHL returned to its roots, when the Edmonton Oilers and Montreal Canadiens played a regular-season game outdoors. The event was so successful that five years later, the Winter Classic was born. Now a New Year's Day tradition, the Winter Classic not only is a fan favorite, but it's also a feat of engineering. In just a few short weeks, an outdoor football or baseball stadium is transformed into a hockey venue for the game.

The 2012 Bridgestone NHL Winter Classic at Citizens Bank Park, home of the Philadelphia Phillies baseball team

Workers construct the rink atop a foundation of wooden planks. Aluminum panels are connected together to form the floor. Underneath, a substance called **glycol** is pumped through pipes from a portable refrigeration truck outside the stadium. The glycol freezes the floor and the 20,000 gallons (75,700 liters) of water that make up the ice.

THE WINTER CLASSIC

YEAR	LOCATION	FIELD TYPE
2008	Ralph Wilson Stadium, Orchard Park, New York	Football
2009	Wrigley Field, Chicago, Illinois	Baseball
2010	Fenway Park, Boston, Massachusetts	Baseball
2011	Heinz Field, Pittsburgh, Pennsylvania	Football
2012	Citizens Bank Park, Philadelphia, Pennsylvania	Baseball

glycol—a kind of antifreeze

FAN EXPERIENCE

Hockey is a fast, hard-hitting, exciting sport. But fans at the games are always looking for more to entertain them. Hockey arenas have turned to technology to give their fans a great experience.

◊ Before the 2012 All-Star Game Weekend, the Scotiabank Place in Ottawa, Ontario, installed a new center-ice scoreboard with a four-sided high-definition video display. The scoreboard is seven times bigger than the old one. Senators fans can't miss many replays with four 331-square-foot (31-square-meter) screens to look at.

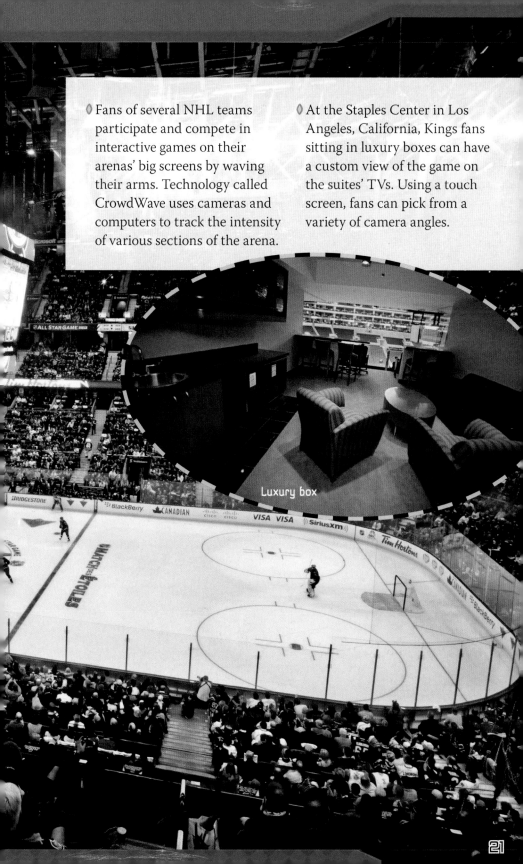

◊ Fans of several NHL teams participate and compete in interactive games on their arenas' big screens by waving their arms. Technology called CrowdWave uses cameras and computers to track the intensity of various sections of the arena.

◊ At the Staples Center in Los Angeles, California, Kings fans sitting in luxury boxes can have a custom view of the game on the suites' TVs. Using a touch screen, fans can pick from a variety of camera angles.

Luxury box

CHAPTER 3

IMPROVING PERFORMANCE

Hockey players must be in tremendous physical shape to play such a demanding sport. They must take care of their bodies year-round through exercise and nutrition in order to survive a long season. NHL teams play 82 regular-season games. If they reach the Stanley Cup Finals, they play 16 to 28 more games.

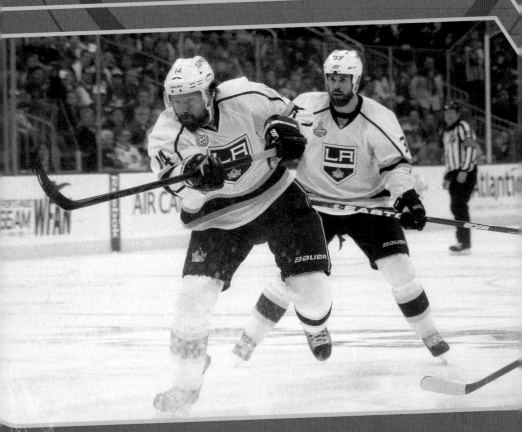

The Los Angeles Kings played 102 games in the 2011–12 season on their way to a Stanley Cup title.

Players don't just work out in the weight room to better themselves. Today they're using computers, sensors, cameras, and radar to try to turn themselves into world-class players. They're even training their brains!

Hockey is a fast sport. Many things happen quickly with 10 skaters and two goalies all on the ice at the same time. Players try to better their focus, their awareness of what's going on around them, and their ability to make snap decisions. To do that, they can use a computer program called IntelliGym. The brain trainer is similar to one used to train fighter pilots.

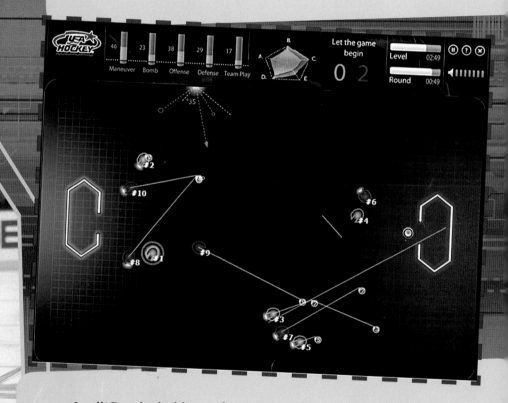

IntelliGym looks like a video game. A player controls a spaceship and tries to shoot a bomb into a goallike opening. On second glance, though, the training software is played much the same way that a hockey game is played. The bomb can be passed from ship to ship. If the player's not careful, the other team of ships can steal the bomb. The game is designed to improve skills important to hockey players, such as focus, attention to detail, and decision-making. After several sessions, many players can anticipate plays, make quicker decisions, and even avoid injuries when they get on the ice.

Hockey players have to work on several skills to make themselves complete players. They have to be slick skaters, strong shooters, and smart passers. While the old saying "Practice makes perfect" is true, practice can also lead to bad habits if players aren't performing those skills correctly.

One way to make sure they're doing it right is by using video **analysis**. Players are filmed as they work out. After the workout session, they can look at the video on a TV or computer monitor to see how they're doing.

Niklas Kronwall (left) and Kyle Quincey (center) of the Detroit Red Wings review video of the previous night's game with the team's video coach, Jay Woodcroft.

To skate efficiently, players need to have proper knee bend and leg drive. They also need to use the edges of their skates, and they need to have good body position and balance. A coach can tell players what they're doing wrong or why they're getting tired quickly. But seeing the video of themselves can help players better understand what the coach is talking about. Then the players can get back on the ice and try again.

analysis—a careful study of something

NO ICE, NO PROBLEM

When Sidney Crosby was young, he shot pucks in his parents' basement in Nova Scotia. When he missed the net, he banged the pucks off the clothes dryer, scarring it with dents and black skid marks. Later he and his friends competed to see who could shoot the most pucks into the dryer. All of that practice helped Sid the Kid start on his path of becoming a great hockey player.

There are many ways hockey players can work on their game outside of a hockey rink. They don't even have to wait until winter to polish their skills. Here are a few inventions that have allowed players to train in their basements, driveways, and garages.

Tiles of a synthetic skating surface are pounded together. The segments have ridges that go together like puzzle pieces.

• Synthetic skating surfaces—These thick, plastic floor tiles are used as a substitute to an ice rink. The tiles allow hockey players to sharpen their blades and actually skate and play hockey.

• Shooting pads and mats—These sheets of high-density polyethylene, a slippery plastic, have an icelike feel for shooters.

• Puck passers—Practicing alone? No problem. These tools feature strong elastic bands that send the puck back to the player to work on passing or shots.

SKATING IN PLACE

Many players work on improving their skating stride, mechanics, and endurance on a skating treadmill. It's not unlike machines used for running or walking. However, it is much larger and its belt is made of synthetic ice.

Users wear a harness to keep from falling down and hurting themselves.

CHECK YOUR HEAD

Injuries are a serious matter, especially in a contact sport like hockey. Concussions are among the most serious.

Rules have changed, penalties have increased, and equipment has been improved to make the game safer for players.

Nathan Horton (18) is checked out by a team trainer after a hard hit.

Many leagues and teams have their players take a computer test called ImPACT before the season begins. The test gives a player a baseline score of how his or her brain is functioning normally. If the player suffers a concussion, he or she retakes the test. The scores are compared to see how bad the concussion is. Then the trainers and doctors determine if and when the player can return to the rink.

ANSWER GRID

▽	≅	√	∠	⊗	×	⇑	/
2	3	4	5	6	7	8	9

TEST GRID

⇑	⊗	×	/	√	≅	√	⊗
8	6	7	9	4	3	4	_

Type in the numbers from the ANSWER GRID into the blank spaces in the TEST GRID.

A hockey player retook a concussion test after a head injury. Trainers compared the results to his baseline score to determine if he was ready to return to the ice.

Some teams are starting to experiment with helmet **sensors** that record the impact of hits. If the shock is high, a signal is sent to a computer or smartphone of a doctor, trainer, or coach. Then the player can immediately be checked for a concussion. If necessary, the player can be removed from the game so he or she doesn't make the injury worse.

FACT

A concussion is a brain injury caused by a sudden blow to or intense shaking of the head that affects brain function.

sensor—device that detects things such as heat, light, sound, or motion, and then reacts to it

CHANGING THE GAME

CHAPTER 4

MAKING SURE IT'S A GOAL

Some call it the War Room. Others call it the Situation Room. Either way, the NHL's video review room is an important one. It's the place where the last word comes down on goal scoring.

The NHL video review room is located in Toronto, Ontario.

The room has a bank of TVs where officials monitor all of the games played on a single night. They have access to many camera angles, including over-the-goal and in-net views. When there's a close play around the net, they determine whether a goal was scored and communicate the result over the phone with the referee on the ice.

For a goal to be scored, it must completely cross the goal line. The puck cannot be put in the net by hand, by a kicking motion, or by a high stick—when the stick is above shoulder height. Video replay tries to ensure that the final call is correct.

A referee talks to NHL officials from the War Room to determine if a last-second goal counted.

FACT

Inventors have experimented with putting sensors in pucks to determine whether the puck completely crossed the line in the net. When the puck crosses a magnetic field over the goal line, a signal is sent, indicating a goal. The same idea would work for calling offsides, when a player crosses the blue line ahead of the puck. The puck would send a signal once it crosses the blue line.

BREAKING DOWN FILM

Fred Shero coached the Philadelphia Flyers to two Stanley Cup championships in the 1970s. While his teams were rough and tough—they were nicknamed the "Broad Street Bullies"—Shero embraced technology. He is one of the first coaches to study film of his teams' and opponents' games.

Members of the Detroit Red Wings review footage from a previous game before practice to help them prepare for the next game.

Today all NHL teams use video coaches or video coordinators. Their job is to watch games on monitors from a special room inside an arena. Using a computer, they mark various points in a game as they happen, including goals, power plays, penalty kills, breakouts, penalties, and hits. Coaches and players can break down and study the clips to get a better understanding of what they're doing right and what they're doing wrong. They can also use the clips to find their opponents' weaknesses.

Brad Richards uses his laptop to stay up-to-date on NHL news.

Thanks to tablet technology, sucha as iPads, each player has 24/7 access to a digital archive of material, such as the player's shifts and plays. Toronto Maple Leafs coach Ron Wilson has even used a tablet and computers on the bench during games to access what his video coach marked for him.

THE STAT CREW

There isn't always a lot of scoring in hockey, but there is a wide variety of statistics. To keep track of a fast-paced game, each team has a staff of workers closely watch the game from the press box. The group must account for all that's happening on the ice, including every hit, shot, turnover, and line change.

Using five computers and a program called H.I.T.S. (Hockey Information and Tracking System), the workers enter data as quickly as they can after it happens. Sports reporters working at the game and even fans checking in from inside and outside the arena can be updated on the action in real time. The stats are available on laptop computers, tablets, and smartphones.

An NCAA referee reviews video replay to determine if the puck passed the goal line.

Meanwhile, official scorers in the press box use video replay, including slow-motion, to make sure goals and assists are awarded correctly. For instance, a replay may show that a defenseman's shot from a point was redirected into the net off the stick of a teammate in front of the net.

LINES OF COMMUNICATION

Even with all of the video and statistical technology available during games, teams still rely on the human eye to figure out what is happening in the rink. Assistant coaches often sit in press boxes high above the ice and act as "eyes in the sky" for their teams. The high angle allows them to see details about breakouts, defensive traps, power plays, and penalty kills.

The press box is the perfect place for assistant coaches to get a better angle of the action.

But how do they relay what they see to the players when they don't want to wait until the period ends? Teams use wireless communication such as microphones and headsets so assistants can talk to one another during the game. The coach in the press box and the video coach in the room under the stands talk to another assistant on the bench. The bench coach can immediately give information to the head coach or instructions to the players.

FACT

Hall of Fame coach Roger Neilson, who coached several teams from 1977 to 2002, is credited as the first coach to use headsets for in-game communication with assistants.

FANS OF THE GAME

CHAPTER 5

BROADCASTING HOCKEY

In 1923 hockey moved out of arenas and into people's homes. That year the first radio broadcast of a game took place. Radio and television have allowed fans to enjoy the game without buying tickets.

Commentators on *NHL Live* discuss the outcome of Game 3 of the Stanley Cup Finals between the New Jersey Devils and Los Angeles Kings.

One of the oldest programs in Canadian broadcasting is *Hockey Night* in Canada. The popular Saturday night games began as a radio show in 1931 as the *General Motors Hockey Broadcast*. The first game featured the Toronto Maple Leafs and the Chicago Blackhawks. Legendary broadcaster Foster Hewitt, the man who coined the phrase, "He shoots, he scores!" announced the game. Two years later games were aired coast to coast, and in 1952 the show moved to television.

The first TV broadcast used three cameras to show the action. Today as many as 16 cameras are used to get fans as close to the action as possible. **Innovations** in high-definition technology and wide-screen televisions have greatly improved viewing from the living room.

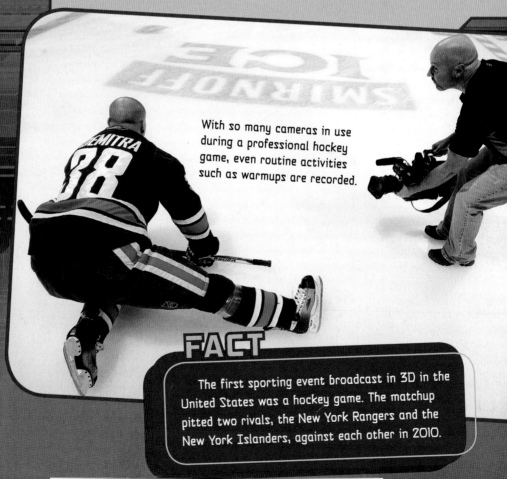

With so many cameras in use during a professional hockey game, even routine activities such as warmups are recorded.

FACT

The first sporting event broadcast in 3D in the United States was a hockey game. The matchup pitted two rivals, the New York Rangers and the New York Islanders, against each other in 2010.

innovation—the creation of new ideas, devices, or methods

CHANGING HOW WE WATCH

Hockey games are watched on more than just television sets. More and more fans are using laptops, tablets, and smartphones to watch their favorite teams. As a result, games have become more interactive.

A fan uses his iPad to record a video of Eric Brewer of the Tampa Bay Lightning as he emerges from the locker room.

Fans are more connected than ever. They chat with one another through Facebook, Twitter, and other social media. They can experience the game together, no matter how far away they are from one another.

The NHL has gotten involved too. Live statistics aren't the only information available during games. If fans go online, they can access live video of the games, including camera angles not available on the TV broadcast. They can chat with professional reporters and hockey experts. They can compete with other fans as they try to predict what will happen in the games. They can even create their own instant replays, including slow-motion clips.

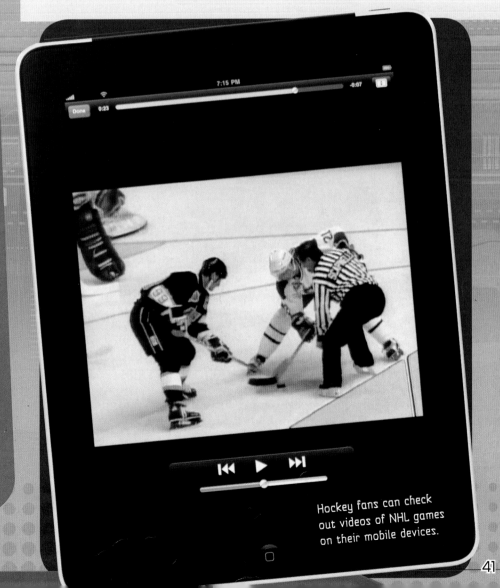

Hockey fans can check out videos of NHL games on their mobile devices.

GOING TOO FAR

Sports broadcasts have improved almost every year. The first sports instant replays were shown in the 1950s during the airing of hockey games. Broadcasters later added on-screen graphics to show the score and the clock. Microphones were used to catch discussions between players, coaches, and referees. In-net cameras looked at goals from various angles. All of those things have helped fans better appreciate the game. But some broadcast experiments have failed.

View from an in-net camera

In 1996 the Fox network tried to improve hockey on TV by making the puck easier to see. On screen the FoxTrax puck glowed with a blue cloud around it. When a player fired a shot over 70 miles (113 km) per hour, a red streak that looked like a comet followed the puck's path toward the net.

To get that look, the pucks were made with special detectors inside. They sent signals to sensors located around the arena. The signals were translated through the network's computer system to give the puck its special appearance on screen.

Some fans didn't like the new puck. Some thought it looked too much like a video game or a cartoon. After two years the glowing puck was no longer used.

THE FUTURE OF HOCKEY

Just like the players of the late 1800s could not have pictured what hockey would look like in the 2000s, it might be hard to predict what the NHL will look like in the 22nd century. Will it be at all similar to today's version of the game? One thing we do know: Technology is always moving forward, and hockey will continue to change.

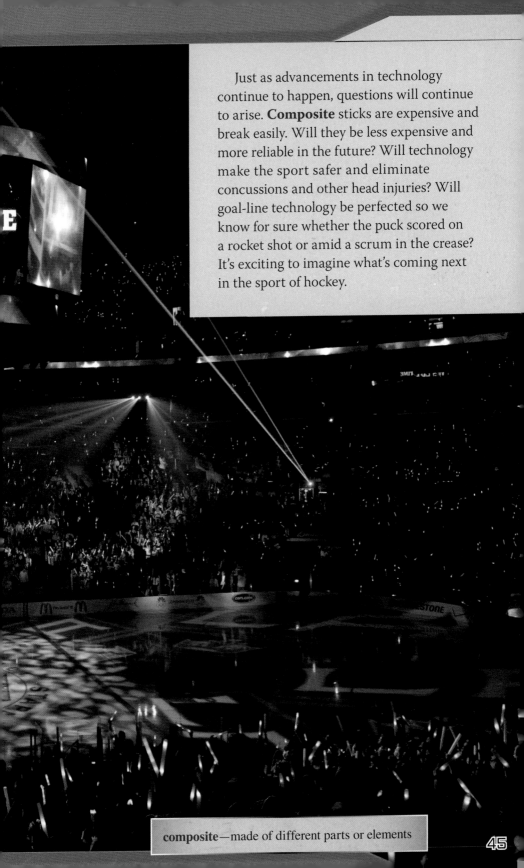

Just as advancements in technology continue to happen, questions will continue to arise. **Composite** sticks are expensive and break easily. Will they be less expensive and more reliable in the future? Will technology make the sport safer and eliminate concussions and other head injuries? Will goal-line technology be perfected so we know for sure whether the puck scored on a rocket shot or amid a scrum in the crease? It's exciting to imagine what's coming next in the sport of hockey.

composite—made of different parts or elements

GLOSSARY

analysis—a careful study of something

breakout—a hockey play to get the puck out of the defensive zone

composite—made of different parts or elements

concussion—an injury to the brain caused by a hit to the head

crease—the area of the ice directly in front of the goal; it's often painted blue

endurance—the ability to keep doing something over a long period of time

forecheck—defensive play while in the offensive zone

glycol—a kind of antifreeze

innovation—the creation of new ideas, devices, or methods

Kevlar—a high-strength material

mechanics—the details about how something works or is done

penalty kill—when a team plays short-handed because a player is in the penalty box

Plexiglas—a strong, clear plastic that can substitute for regular glass

power play—when a team has a one- or two-player advantage because the other team has players in the penalty box

sensor—device that detects things such as heat, light, sound, or motion, and then reacts to it

synthetic—not natural, made by combining different substances

titanium—a very strong and light metal

trap—a defensive style of play, often done in the neutral zone

READ MORE

Biskup, Agnieszka. *Hockey: How it Works.* The Science of Sports. Mankato, Minn.: Capstone Press, 2010.

Ross, Stewart. *Higher, Further, Faster: Is Technology Improving Sport?* TechKnow. Hoboken, N.J.: Wiley, 2008.

Thomas, Keltie. *How Hockey Works: The Science of Hockey.* Berkeley, Calif.: Owlkids, 2010.

INTERNET SITES

FactHound offers a safe, fun way to find Internet sites related to this book. All of the sites on FactHound have been researched by our staff.

Here's all you do:

Visit *www.facthound.com*

Type in this code: 9781429699549

Super-cool stuff!

Check out projects, games and lots more at
www.capstonekids.com

INDEX